Don't Look Down
on the
DEFILEMENTS
They Will Laugh At You

ASHIN TEJANIYA

DON'T LOOK DOWN ON THE DEFILEMENTS

Third US Edition, November 2015

This is a gift of Dhamma and must not be sold. You may make photocopies for your own use or to give away to friends. Kindly ask for permission from Ashin Tejaniya first before doing any translations on this book. For more dhamma materials and contact information, please visit: www.ashintejaniya.org

ISBN 978-0-9835844-0-7

This printing of 3,000 copies on November 2015 for free distribution by:

Wisdom Streams Foundation
www.wisdomstreams.org
info@wisdomstreams.org

To support future printing of dhamma books for free distribution, donations can be made to "Wisdom Streams Foundation" at www.wisdomstreams.org/dana or by mail to:

Wisdom Streams Foundation
c/o Sajama
2223 Grant Street
Berkeley, CA 94703

Thank you for your support.

Printed with permission of Ashin Tejaniya with layout assistance from Hor Tuck Loon (Malaysia).

May all beings be happy!

NAMO TASSA BHAGAVATO
ARAHATO
SAMMĀ-SAMBUDDHASSA

Homage to Him, the Blessed One,
the Worthy One,
the Perfectly Self-Enlightened One

Acknowledgements

My special gratitude goes to my teacher, the late Venerable Shwe Oo Min Sayadaw Bhaddanta Kosalla Mahā Thera, who taught me Dhamma and the right attitude for my spiritual development and meditation practice.

I want to express my appreciation to all yogis. Their questions and difficulties have inspired many of the explanations and answers given in this book. I really hope that this book will help yogis to better understand mindfulness meditation and to deepen their practice.

Finally, I would like to thank everyone who has contributed to the completion of this book.

Ashin Tejaniya
Myanmar

Contents

What are Defilements?

Defilements are not only the gross manifestations of greed, hatred, and delusion but also all their friends and relatives, even the very distant ones!! See if you have ever had one of the following – or similar – thoughts cross your mind:

"Those lights should not be on at this time of the day!" "His behaviour is so irritating." "He should not have done that." "I could do it a lot faster." "I am a hopeless meditator; my mind cannot even stay on the rising-falling for one minute." "Yesterday my meditation was so good; today I am all over the place." "Wow, this was a wonderful sit; now I need to be really mindful so I don't lose this feeling." "I must stay in the Dhamma hall; others will think I am lazy if I don't." "I need an extra portion of potatoes today because it's good for my health." "Yuk! The salad has onions in it." "No bananas again!" "He is so selfish, so inconsiderate." "Why is this happening to me?" "Who is responsible for cleaning the toilets?" "Why is this yogi walking here?" "They shouldn't be making so much noise!" "There are too many people here; I can't meditate." "Someone is sitting in my seat!" "She is so pretty!" "He walks so elegantly!"

All such thoughts are motivated by defilements!! Don't underestimate them!

Have you ever told someone you were not angry even though you clearly did not like what he had done? Do you sometimes talk negatively about your boss, a member of your family, or even a good friend? Do you occasionally tell a dirty joke? Do you habitually sweet talk people into doing things for you? Do you automatically raise your voice when someone does not agree with your point of view?

All such talk is motivated by defilements! Watch out for it!

Have you ever knocked really hard on someone's door, or refused to enter a room simply because someone you dislike was in there, or jumped a queue, or used the shampoo someone left in the bathroom, or made a private call using your employer's phone line, or done any similar actions – all sort of unthinkingly?

All such actions are motivated by defilements! Become aware of them.

Dear Reader

This is not a complete or systematic description of a meditation method. We simply want to share with you practical aspects of this approach to meditation. The advice given on the following pages is based on Ashin Tejaniya's meditation and teaching experience. We hope you will find it helpful for your own practice, but people are different and that is why there are so many different ways to develop mindfulness. We have found that this particular approach works best for us and we would like to encourage you to give it a try. The information given reflects our understanding and interpretation of this approach. Of course you will have difficulties or questions which we have not addressed at all in this book – you need to bring these up in Dhamma discussions (see chapter **Dhamma Discussions**).

When you read this book, please do not cling to dictionary definitions. For example, for our purposes, the words 'watching', 'observing', 'being mindful', 'paying attention' and 'being aware' are used interchangeably. 'Awareness' and 'mindfulness' also mean the same. 'Understanding', 'realization', 'insight', and 'wisdom' are used to express something similar, and the word 'object' is often used to mean 'experience'. 'Sensations' refers to bodily sensations and 'feelings' to mental feelings. We also describe several key points of this approach from various angles and in different contexts. Our experience has shown that such repetition is very helpful, particularly for those new to mindfulness meditation.

We have tried to translate and express Ashin Tejaniya's teachings and ideas as accurately as possible. However, we may have made mistakes and it is likely that some details got lost in translation.

Interpreter, Ghostwriter, and *Editors*

Mindfulness Meditation
(Satipaṭṭhāna)

At this centre we practise mindfulness meditation (Satipaṭṭhāna). However before we start practising we must know how to practise. We need to have the right information and the right idea about the nature of the practice so that we have the right attitude when we practise.

We meditate on the Four Foundations of Mindfulness (body, feelings, mind, and dhamma). As the practice develops we give more and more emphasis to the mind because meditation is the work of the mind.

What follows below should be sufficient to get you started. Later on, Dhamma discussions will take you deeper into the practice. Please read and re-read this guidance slowly and carefully.

MIND WORK

Meditation is mind work, the work of being aware. It is not the work of the body. It is not what you do with your body, the way you sit, walk, or move. Meditation is experiencing the mind and the body directly, moment to moment, with the right understanding.

When, for example, you put your hands together and pay attention, you will feel and be aware of that sensation – that's the mind at work. Can you know those touching sensations if you are thinking of other things? You obviously cannot. You have to be attentive. When you pay attention to your body you will notice many sensations. Can you feel the different qualities of these sensations? Do you need labeling in order to bring your attention and awareness to the different sensations? You certainly do not. In fact, labeling will prevent you from being able to observe details. Simply be aware! However, being aware is only one part of meditation.

In addition, you also need to have the right information and a clear understanding of the practice to work with awareness intelligently. Right now you are reading this book in order to understand mindfulness meditation. This information will work at the back of your mind when you meditate. Reading or discussing

Dhamma, and reflecting on how to practice are all mind work, are all part of meditation.

Continuity is vital for this practice, for meditative mind work. You need to remind yourself to be aware all day long. So watch yourself everywhere, all the time; when sitting, walking, cleaning, talking, anything you do – watch it, know it, be aware of what is going on.

RELAX

When doing mind work, you should be relaxed and practise without tension, without forcing yourself. The more relaxed you are, the easier it is to develop mindfulness. We do not tell you to 'focus', 'concentrate', or 'penetrate' because it suggests the use of excessive energy. Instead we encourage you to 'observe', 'watch', 'be aware', or 'pay attention'.

If you are tense or find yourself getting tense, relax. There is no need to make a forceful effort. Right now, are you aware of your posture? Are you aware of your hands touching this book? Can you feel your feet? Notice how little energy or effort you need to know any of this! That is all the energy you need to remain aware, but remember, you need to do this all day long. If you practise this way, your energy will increase over the day. If you use excessive energy, if the mind wastes energy, you will get tired. In order to be able to practise continuously, you just need to keep reminding yourself to be aware. This right effort will allow you to practise in a relaxed way, free of tension. If the mind is too tense or too tired, you cannot learn anything. If the mind and the body are getting tired, something is wrong with the way you are practising. Check your posture; check the way you are meditating. Are you comfortable and alert? Also check your attitude; don't practise with a mind that wants something or wants something to happen. The result will only be that you tire yourself.

So you must know whether you are feeling tense or relaxed. Check this repeatedly throughout the day. If you feel tense, observe the tension; if you don't do this, tension will grow (see last paragraph in DAILY ACTIVITIES). Once you feel relaxed, you can meditate more easily.

RIGHT ATTITUDE (yoniso manasikāra)

Being relaxed and aware is essential but it is also very important to have the right attitude, the right frame of mind. What does having the right attitude mean? Having the right attitude is a way of looking at things that makes you content, comfortable, and feel at ease with whatever you are experiencing. Wrong ideas, wrong information, or ignorance of the defilements affect your attitude.

We all have wrong attitudes; we cannot help having them. So do not try to have the right attitude, try to recognize if you have the wrong or the right attitude instead. It is important to be aware when you have right attitudes, but it is even more important to recognize and investigate your wrong attitudes. Try to understand your wrong attitudes; find out how they affect your practice, and see how they make you feel. So watch yourself and keep checking to see what state of mind you are practising with.

Right attitude allows you to accept, acknowledge, and observe whatever is happening – whether pleasant or unpleasant – in a relaxed and alert way. You have to accept and watch both good and bad experiences. Every experience, whether good or bad, gives you a learning opportunity to notice whether the mind accepts things the way they are, or whether it likes, dislikes, reacts, or judges.

Liking something means you desire it, disliking something means you have an aversion to it. Desire and aversion are defilements that arise out of ignorance – ignorance or delusion is a defilement too. So do not try to create anything; trying to create something is greed. Do not reject what is happening; rejecting what is happening is aversion. Not knowing that something is happening or has stopped happening is delusion.

You are not trying to make things turn out the way you want them to happen. You are trying to know what is happening as it is. Thinking things should be this way or that, wanting this or that to happen or not to happen is expectation. Expectations create anxiety and can lead to aversion. It is important that you become aware of your attitudes!

It is a wrong attitude to judge the practice and become dissatisfied with the way it is going. The dissatisfaction either arises from the idea that things are not the way we think they should be, from a desire that they should be different, or from ignorance of what right practice is. These attitudes close the mind and hinder the practice. Try to recognize dissatisfaction, to fully accept it, and to watch it very alertly. During this process of observation and exploration of the experience of dissatisfaction, its causes could become clear. Understanding the causes will dissolve the dissatisfaction and will help you to recognize them if they come up again. You will see more and more clearly the harm dissatisfaction causes to the mind and the body. You will become more mindful of your judgmental attitudes and gradually abandon them. In this way you are developing skills in dealing with defilements.

Wrong attitudes are caused by delusion. We all have them in our minds. All wrong attitudes are the defilements craving and aversion or any of their relatives such as elation, sadness, or worry. Not accepting defilements will only strengthen them. The defilements hinder your progress in meditation and prevent you from living your life fully. They also prevent you from finding true peace and freedom. Don't look down on the defilements; they will laugh at you!

Look out for the defilements. Get to know the defilements that arise in your mind. Observe and try to understand them. Do not attach to them, reject, or ignore them, and do not identify with them. As you stop attaching to or identifying with the defilements their strength will slowly diminish. You have to keep double checking to see what attitude you are meditating with.

Always bear in mind that mindfulness meditation is a learning process during which you get to know the mind and body relationship. Just be natural and simple; there is no need to slow down unnaturally. You simply want to see things as they are.

There is no need to make an effort to concentrate. Concentration will naturally grow with practice. Our objective is to become more and more mindful. The more continuous your mindfulness is, the sharper and more receptive the mind becomes.

Don't forget: the object is not really important; the observing mind that is working in the background to be aware is of real importance. If the observing is done with the right attitude, any object is the right object. Do you have the right attitude?

BE AWARE INTELLIGENTLY

Mindfulness meditation is more than just observing things with a receptive mind. You cannot practise it blindly, mechanically, without thinking. You have to use both knowledge and intelligence to bring your practice to life.

The main tools you need to be aware intelligently are:

- the right information and a clear understanding of the practice,
- the right motivation or interest, and
- the right thinking, reflection, or inquiry.

Right information and clear understanding of the practice is what you gain from reading relevant texts and from Dhamma discussions. The right motivation or interest is based on clearly knowing why you are practising here and now. Have you ever asked yourself questions like: "Why do I want to meditate?" "What do I expect to gain?" "Do I understand what meditation means?" Right motivation and interest will grow out of your answers to these questions. Right information and right motivation will have a strong influence on the way you think or reflect when practising. They enable you to ask intelligent questions at the right moment.

Right thinking, reflection, or inquiry is thinking that helps you to practise correctly. If, as a beginner, you are faced with a particular situation in your practice, you should first reflect on what the instructions on dealing with such a situation are, and then try to apply them. If it is not clear to you what is going on, you could also ask yourself questions such as: "What is my attitude?" "Which defilement am I dealing with?" However, make sure you do not think or reflect too much, especially if you are a beginner; your mind might wander off. Such questions or thoughts should only serve to heighten your interest.

Even if you have the right information, the right motivation and made the right reflections you could still make mistakes. Recognizing mistakes is an important aspect of being aware intelligently. We all make mistakes; it is natural to do so. If you find you have made a mistake, accept and acknowledge it; try to learn from it.

As your mindfulness becomes more and more continuous, your interest in the practice will grow. Being aware intelligently will help you to deepen your practice, to come to new understandings. Ultimately, it will help you to fulfil the objective of mindfulness meditation: vipassanā insights.

Mindfulness meditation is a learning process; use your awareness intelligently!

POSTURES / EATING / DAILY ACTIVITIES

Don't forget to watch yourself from the time you wake up until the time you fall asleep. Whenever you notice that you have not been mindful, check the state of your mind. Try to feel what mood the mind is in. Are you relaxed or not? Then start by observing some obvious sensations on any part of the body. The meditating mind must be simple, not complicated. You can use any sensation as the main object to bring the mind to the present moment. The main or primary object helps you to keep the mind aware, in the present moment. It is something you can always go to when you are not sure what to observe. However, you do not have to stay with that main object all the time. It is perfectly alright if the mind's attention moves to other objects such as sensations, hearing, even a wandering mind, as long as you are aware that the mind is now aware of these new objects. It is also fine if it knows several objects at the same time.

In sitting meditation both the mind and the body should be comfortable. Keep checking whether you are relaxed or not. If there is tension, first relax, then check your attitude. If there is resistance, feel the resistance and observe it. Be simple and just watch what is happening. Watch whatever the mind is aware of – your posture, bodily sensations, your breathing, feelings and emotions, the wandering or thinking mind, hearing or smelling. If you are sitting comfortably on your cushion and are busy thinking about something very important without even realizing that there is thinking going on, you are not meditating! When you suddenly realize that this is happening, do not worry about it. Relax, check your attitude, i.e. start this whole exercise again from the beginning.

Be aware that you are walking whenever you walk. You do not need to walk fast or slowly, just walk at a natural pace. You can watch what the mind pays attention to, or just have an overall feel of the sensation of your whole body walking. If the mind settles on particular sensations or body movements, that is alright too. But remember, you do not have to focus on one object continuously; in fact you should avoid doing this if it makes you tense. You can also notice hearing and that you are looking to see where you are going. Try not to look around as it will distract you. However, once your mindfulness has become more continuous, you need to learn to be aware whenever you look at something. This ability to be aware of seeing comes with practice. As long as you are not skilful at this, seeing will tend to distract you, make you lose your mindfulness.

When you do standing meditation you can follow the same basic principles as in sitting and walking meditation. Keep checking for tension!

When you eat, do not hurry. When you are eager to eat you will lose mindfulness. So if you become aware that you are eating quickly, stop eating and watch the eagerness or the feelings that accompany it for a while. You need to be reasonably calm to find out what the process of eating is like. Experience the sensations, the smells, the tastes, the mental states, what you like and dislike. Also notice bodily movements. Do not worry about observing every detail, just remain aware of your experience.

Your personal time and activities are also very important times to be mindful. You tend to lose your mindfulness most easily when you are on your own. Are you aware when you close doors, brush your teeth, put on your clothes, take a shower, go to toilet? How do you feel when you do these activities? Do you notice what you like and what you dislike? Are you aware when you are looking at something? Are you aware when you are listening to something? Are you aware when you have judgments about what you see, hear, smell, taste, touch, think, or feel? Are you aware when you are talking? Are you aware of the tone and loudness of your voice?

It is important that you regularly check whether you are relaxed or tense; if you don't, you will not be aware whether you are relaxed or getting tense. When you find yourself tense, watch the tension. You cannot practise when the mind is tense. If you get tense, it indicates that your mind is not working in the right way. Inquire into the way your mind has been working. If you do this often enough during the day you may prevent a buildup of tension. With practice you may also become aware of the reason for your tension. Do not forget to observe tension! If you become tense easily, do lying down meditation once a day. This will also help you to practise awareness in every posture you are in.

WANDERING MIND / SOUNDS

When the mind is thinking or wandering, when a sound keeps catching your attention, just be aware of it. Thinking is a natural activity of the mind. It is natural that, if you have good hearing, you will hear sounds. You are doing well if you are aware that the mind is thinking or hearing. But if you feel disturbed by thoughts or sounds, or if you have a reaction or judgment to them, there is a problem with your attitude. The wandering mind and sounds are not the problem; your attitude that 'they should not be around' is the problem. So understand that you have just become aware of some functions of the mind. These too are just objects for your attention.

Thinking is a mental activity. When you are new to this practice you should not try to watch thinking continuously. Neither should you try to avoid observing thoughts by immediately going to your primary meditation object. When you realize that you are thinking, always pay attention to the thought first and then remind yourself that a thought is just a thought. Do not think of it as 'my thought'. Now you can return to your primary meditation object.

When you feel disturbed by the thinking mind, remind yourself that you are not practising to prevent thinking, but rather to recognize and acknowledge thinking whenever it arises. If you are not aware, you cannot know that you are thinking. The fact that you recognize that you are thinking means that you are aware. Remember that it does not matter how many times the mind thinks, wanders off, or gets annoyed about something – as long as you become aware of it.

It does not matter whether thinking stops or not. It is more important that you understand whether your thoughts are skilful, unskilful, appropriate, inappropriate, necessary or unnecessary. This is why it is essential to learn to watch thinking without getting involved. When a thought keeps growing no matter how much effort you put into trying to simply observe it, you are probably somehow involved in the thought. When this happens, when thinking becomes so incessant that you can no longer observe it, stop looking at the thoughts and try to watch the underlying feelings or bodily sensations instead.

No matter whether you are sitting, walking, or going about your daily activities, ask yourself now and again: What is the mind doing? Thinking? Thinking about what? Being aware? Being aware of what?

PAIN / UNPLEASANT SENSATIONS / EMOTIONS

When you experience pains, aches and other bodily discomforts, it means you have a mental resistance to them and therefore you are not ready yet to observe these unpleasant physical sensations directly. Nobody likes pain and if you observe it while still feeling any resistance towards it, it will become worse. It is like when you are angry with someone; if you look at that person again and again you will become even angrier. So never force yourself to observe pain; this is not a fight, this is a learning opportunity. You are not observing pain to lessen it or to make it go away. You are observing it – especially your mental reactions to it – in order to understand the connection between your mental reactions and your perception of the physical sensations.

Check your attitude first. Wishing for the pain to decrease or go away is the wrong attitude. It does not matter whether the pain goes away or not. Pain is not the problem; your negative mental reaction to it is the problem. If the pain is caused by some kind of injury you should of course be careful not to make things worse, but if you are well and healthy, pain is simply an important opportunity to practise watching the mind at work. When there is pain, the mental feelings and reactions are strong and therefore easy to observe. Learn to watch anger or resistance, tension or discomfort in your mind. If necessary, alternate between checking your feelings and the attitude behind your resistance. Keep reminding yourself to relax the mind and the body, and observe how it affects your mental resistance. There is a direct link between your state of mind and pain. The more relaxed and calm the observing mind, the less intense you will perceive the pain to be. Of course, if your mind reacts strongly to the pain (i.e. if you experience pain as unbearable) you should change your posture and make yourself comfortable.

So if you want to learn how to deal with pain skilfully, try this: From the moment you start feeling pain, no matter how weak it is, check your mind and body for tension, and relax. Part of your mind will remain aware of the pain. So check for tension again and again, and relax. Also check your attitude and keep reminding yourself that you have the choice to change your posture if you experience too much pain, as this will make the mind more willing to work with it. Keep repeating this until you no longer feel you want to watch the tension, the fear, the desire to get up, or the unwillingness to stay with the pain. Now you should change your posture.

When you are able to bear with pain, it does not mean that you are equanimous. Most of us start off by trying hard to sit for a fixed period of time, forcing ourselves not to move. If we succeed to sit for that full hour we feel great, otherwise we feel we have failed. We usually try to bear the pain longer and longer, i.e. we work on increasing our threshold of pain. However, in this process we neglect watching the mind and we are not really aware of our mental reactions to the pain. We fail to realize that developing a high threshold of pain does not mean that the mind is not reacting to the pain.

If you stop forcing yourself to sit for a fixed period of time and instead start watching the mental reactions in the ways described above, your resistance to the pain will gradually decrease and your mind will become more equanimous. Understanding the difference between equanimity and being able to bear with pain is really important. Mindfulness meditation is not about forcing but about understanding. Real equanimity is the result of true understanding of the nature of liking and disliking through observation and investigation.

It is best to look at pain directly only if you cannot feel a resistance to it. Keep in mind that there may be a reaction at a subtle level. As soon as you recognize mental discomfort, turn your attention to that feeling. If you can see subtle mental discomfort, watch it change; does it increase or decrease? As the mind becomes more equanimous and sensitive it will recognize subtle reactions more easily. When you look at mental discomfort at a more subtle level you may get to the point when your mind feels completely equanimous. If you look at pain directly and if there is true equanimity, mental discomfort will not arise any-more.

Remember that you are not looking at the reactions of the mind to make them go away. Always take reactions as an opportunity to investigate their nature. Ask yourself questions! How do they make you feel? What thoughts are in your mind? How does what you think affect the way you feel? How does what you feel affect the way you think? What is the attitude behind the thoughts? How does any of this change the way you perceive pain?

Try to apply the relevant points mentioned above to deal with any other physical discomforts such as itching, and feeling hot or cold. Moreover, whatever skills we learn in dealing with our reactions to physical discomforts can also be applied in dealing with defilements such as emotions of anger, frustration, jealousy, disappointment, or rejection as well as happiness, pleasure, lust or attachment. They and all their relatives – even their distant ones – should be dealt with in similar ways as pain. You need to learn to recognize and let go of both attachment and aversion.

When you investigate such emotions, it is important that you remind yourself that they are natural phenomena. They are not 'your' emotions; everybody experiences them. You always need to keep this in mind when you examine the thoughts and mental images that accompany emotions. All thoughts you identify with actually 'fuel' the emotions.

However, when the emotion you experience is very strong, you might not be able to look at the accompanying thoughts without getting even more emotional. In such a case, it is usually best to first become very clearly aware of and look at the pleasant or unpleasant feelings and sensations that accompany the emotion. But if you find even looking at these feelings and sensations too overwhelming, you could turn your attention to a neutral or pleasant object, for example your breath or a sound. Doing this will skilfully distract the mind and stop it from thinking – or will at least reduce thinking. 'You' will no longer be so involved in the 'story' and therefore the emotion will subside. But do not completely ignore those feelings and sensations; take a look at them every now and then!

When a strong emotion has subsided, or when you are looking at a weak emotion, you will be able to look at the feelings, the thoughts plus the bodily sensations. The better you understand how they all interrelate, the more skilfully and effectively you will be able to handle any kind of emotion.

Don't forget to check your attitude: Check to see whether you really accept the emotion or whether you have a resistance towards it. Any unnoticed resistance to and any unnoticed identification with the emotion will 'feed' it, will make it grow bigger (snowball effect). Remember that the emotions do not need to go away at all. The objective is to know what the emotions feel like, to know what you are thinking when there are emotions, and to understand their 'nature' and the mind's behaviour.

CONTINUITY OF AWARENESS

You need to be aware of yourself continuously, whatever posture you are in, from the time you wake up until you fall asleep. Do not let your mind become idle or run freely. It is important that the mind keeps working, i.e. keeps being aware. Whatever you do, it is the awareness that is important. Continuity of awareness requires right effort. In our context, right effort means to keep reminding yourself to be aware. Right effort is persistent effort. It is not energy used to focus hard on something. It is effort which is simply directed at remaining aware, which should not require much energy.

You do not need to know every detail of your experience. Just be aware and know what you are aware of. Ask yourself often: "What am I aware of now?" "Am I properly aware or only superficially aware?" This will support continuity of mindfulness. Remember: it is not difficult to be aware – it is just difficult to do it continuously!

Momentum is important to strengthen your practice and this can only be achieved with continuity of mindfulness. With continuous right effort, mindfulness will slowly gain momentum and become stronger. When mindfulness has momentum, the mind is strong. A strong mind has right mindfulness, right concentration, and wisdom.

Make a consistent effort. Keep reminding yourself to be mindful and your mindfulness will become more and more continuous.

WHY?

At this point you might feel overwhelmed by all the information that you have been asked to bear in mind while you meditate. Why do you need to know so much before you even start practising? Giving you all this information, all these suggestions and all this advice basically serves one purpose only: to give you the right view or the right understanding that helps you to meditate with the right attitude. When you have the right understanding you will naturally apply the right effort and develop right mindfulness and wisdom. The information you have accumulated and understood forms the basis for the views that you hold, and these influence the way the mind naturally operates in any situation.

ESSENCE OF THE PRACTICE

Develop a right understanding of the practice.

•

Practise continuously; it is absolutely essential for the development of your practice.

•

Relax!

•

Have the right attitude;
accept your experience just as it is.

•

Be aware intelligently.

•

Recognize the defilements.

Dhamma Discussions

Dhamma discussions or meditation interviews give you an opportunity to share your meditation experiences with your teacher and get some advice.

The teacher wants to know how you are doing – whether you are able to be relaxed and aware, whether your awareness is continuous, whether you can recognize your wrong and right attitudes, whether you can recognize and observe your reactions, how you feel, what you have understood, etc. Such information forms the basis for Dhamma discussions; only if the teacher knows your strengths and weaknesses can he give you proper guidance for your practice.

You can talk about where you are at and where you would like to be. You have to be true to yourself. If you report only on your good or only on your bad experiences, it will be difficult to give you the advice you need.

Mindfulness Gains Momentum

When you are new to the practice you will have to remind yourself often to be aware. At first you will be rather slow in noticing that you have lost awareness and probably think that it is fairly continuous. But once your awareness becomes sharper, you will begin to notice that you actually lose it quite often. You might even get the impression that your awareness is getting worse when in fact you are just becoming more often aware of losing awareness. This is a step in the right direction. It shows that your awareness is getting better. So never give yourself a hard time, simply accept where you are at and keep reminding yourself to be aware.

Just reminding yourself to be aware or mindful, however, is not enough. In order for mindfulness to become stronger you also need to have the right attitude, to have an observing mind free from defilements. Observing becomes difficult if, for example, you are worried about your progress. First you need to become aware that this is a defilement and then make it your object of observation. Whenever you experience doubt, uneasiness, dissatisfaction, tension, frustration or elation, look at them. Examine them, ask yourself questions such as: "What kinds of thoughts are in my mind?" "What is my attitude?" This will help you to understand how the defilements affect you. You need patience, interest, and a sense of curiosity to do this. As you gradually become more skilful at observing with the right attitude, mindfulness will become stronger and more continuous. This will help you gain more confidence in your practice.

At this point you will start seeing benefits and the practice of mindfulness will become less work and more fun. You will find it easier to remind yourself to be mindful and to spot the defilements. As a result, mindfulness will become even more continuous and over time, as the practice matures, mindfulness will gain momentum.

Once your practice has momentum, you will remain aware naturally. This natural awareness has an almost tangible feel to it and gives you a sense of freedom you have never experienced before. You simply always know when it is there and you experience it most of the time. In other words, you are aware of the awareness, the mind becomes an object of awareness. When you have this kind of momentum, the mind becomes more equanimous.

Now awareness will be strong and you will need very little effort to sustain its momentum. You will always be aware of several different objects without conscious effort. For example, while washing your hands you will probably notice movement, the touch and smell of the soap, the sensation and the sound of the running water. While knowing all this you might become aware of the sensation of your feet touching the floor, hearing the loudspeakers blaring from the monastery across the field, or seeing stains on the wall and feeling an urge to wipe them off. While all this is happening you might also be aware of any liking or disliking. Every time you wash your hands you are of course likely to be aware of different objects. Natural awareness is constantly shifting, constantly sweeping around, letting go of some objects and taking in other objects, shifting from one set of objects to another.

When you have natural awareness it might feel as though things have slowed down since you can now take in so many different objects, whereas at the beginning of the practice you struggled to be aware of only one or two objects. However, you can still lose your balance quite suddenly when you unexpectedly experience the stronger forms of greed or anger. The difference is that now the mind usually spots gross defilements or wrong attitudes very quickly and they will then either dissolve immediately or at least immediately start losing their strength. You will still lose awareness, the mind can still wander off or awareness can fade, but you usually become aware of this quite soon, i.e. natural awareness snaps back into action.

Before you get too excited though, here is a word of warning. It is not easy to get this kind of momentum. You cannot make it happen. You need to be patient. It is possible to experience momentum after meditating full time for only a few weeks but it will not last very long. Maintaining momentum takes skill and practice. When you first get it you are likely to lose it again within hours or minutes even. Never try to get it back; this can only happen naturally, simply through persistent practice. Most people will take many months or years to acquire the necessary skills and understanding to have natural awareness throughout the day.

When your practice has momentum, concentration naturally becomes better, i.e. the mind is more stable. The mind also becomes sharper, more content, more simple and honest, more flexible, and more sensitive. It can usually spot the subtle defilements quite easily and yet still remain aware of other objects. Natural mindfulness not only enables you to be aware of many different objects, it also enables you to understand cause and effect, to observe details and to deal effectively with more subtle defilements.

You might, for example, feel quite relaxed and calm while walking to the meditation hall and then notice subtle restlessness during sitting meditation. The mind is now aware of the defilement, accepts the experience and starts getting interested. The question "Why is there restlessness?" will probably come up. The mind then simply stays with this question. At the same time you also explore any thoughts, feelings and physical tensions which you know are somehow connected to the restlessness. Then, suddenly you might understand that it is an accumulation of small incidences of stress, frustration, or elation that lies behind this restlessness and the physical tension. In other words, wisdom starts sorting things out. As the mind now understands the causes for the restlessness, it immediately starts getting weaker and the tension in the body starts softening up too.

If you continue observing you might discover that some restlessness and some tension still remain. The question "Why did those incidences happen?" might come up and bring you a step further. You might see the unnoticed wants, resistances, views, hopes or expectations that led to these incidences. Since you now see the 'original' causes for your restlessness, your mind can let go of it completely.

Since the mind has become aware of the causes for this restlessness and tension, it will be on the lookout for similar kinds of incidences that lead to stress, frustration, or elation. When they come up again, wisdom will spot the defilements behind them. This way mindfulness becomes even more continuous, the mind even stronger. Now faith, effort, mindfulness, concentration, and wisdom work very closely together. In other words, the Dhamma is doing its own work.

However, even natural mindfulness cannot always recognize defilements. We all have our blind spots, ingrained habit patterns which we are not aware of. Natural mindfulness will not be able to see blind spots. They are deeply hidden in the mind and therefore inaccessible to direct observation. What mindfulness can see though are emotional reactions in other people. So whenever you notice that people around you become defensive in some way, reflect on your behaviour and your attitude. Usually, however, it will not become clear to you how you could possibly have offended the other person. If you feel comfortable with the person you seem to have upset, you could ask for feedback. Otherwise it is best to describe the situation to a good friend to see whether he or she is aware of your shortcoming in this area. Once you know your problem you could also bring it up in Dhamma discussions. It is important to uncover and explore such hidden habits. Only if you are aware of the wrong attitudes that cause 'blind' habits, will wisdom become able to look out for them.

When you are new to the practice you have to make an effort to bring wisdom into play. You have to use your mindfulness intelligently in order to practice effectively. Particularly when you come across difficulties you have to think of ways to deal with the situation. Over time though, as mindfulness becomes more continuous, wisdom starts coming in more quickly to do its work. Wisdom knows the difference between wrong and right attitude, wisdom dissolves the defilements. When your practice gains momentum, mindfulness and wisdom start working together. When mindfulness has become natural, the wisdom you have acquired is always available.

No matter how often you lose mindfulness, always gently and patiently bring yourself to the present moment. Remind yourself persistently to be aware but never be eager for progress. Never mind if others seem to progress much faster than you; you are walking your own path at your own speed. All you need to do is persevere and sooner or later mindfulness will naturally gain momentum.

Wisdom

We usually acquire wisdom or knowledge by learning through reading or hearing (*sutamayā paññā*), by thinking and reasoning (*cintāmayā paññā*), and through direct experience (*bhāvanāmayā paññā*).

Sutamayā paññā is acquiring the right information to get us started. Cintāmayā paññā is the process of digesting this information. Bhāvanāmayā paññā is understanding which arises through direct experience. We need both sutamayā paññā and cintāmayā paññā in order to practice mindfulness effectively so that experiential wisdom, bhāvanāmayā paññā, can arise. All three are part of meditation, all of them are essential for vipassanā.

When we are new to meditation we need to read Dhamma books or at least listen to and participate in Dhamma discussions. This gives us the information and advice we need to practise, some 'material' to think about. We need to remember information and advice, we need to reflect when confronted with difficulties, and – of course – we should also ask questions in Dhamma discussions.

Making this conscious effort to bring in wisdom is essential. However, it is also very important to bear in mind the impact that this acquired knowledge will have on our practice. All such information will keep working at the back of our minds, will influence the way we think, the way we see things. So make sure that you have really understood 'the basics'; make sure that you know what you are doing. Whenever you are uncertain or when you cannot figure things out by yourself, clarify your understanding with a teacher. It is vital to have the right information, the right motivation and the right thinking to practise intelligently and effectively. For most of us this process of acquiring wisdom is a slow and often painful learning experience – we keep making mistakes.

Don't be afraid of making mistakes and – even more importantly – never feel bad about having made a mistake. We cannot avoid making mistakes; they are in a sense the stepping stones of our path, of our progress. Becoming aware of, carefully looking at, and learning from mistakes is wisdom at work! As we learn from our mistakes, wisdom will start coming in more naturally, more automatically. Over the years, as our practice progresses, as we become more and more mindful, the knowledge and understanding we have accumulated will naturally come in more quickly. Wisdom and mindfulness will start working as a team.

When awareness becomes natural, the mind is strong and the wisdom you have acquired is always available. You no longer need to make an effort to bring it in. When the observing mind gets stronger, wisdom can deal more competently with defilements. As your wisdom grows, the mind becomes purer and more equanimous. Eventually you will start experiencing moments of equanimity and clarity in which you begin to see things in a completely new light. In other words, you start having insights.

Having an insight means understanding deeply what you previously only understood superficially, intellectually. It is something that happens naturally, spontaneously; you cannot make it happen. The account of someone describing certain experiences leading up to an insight and the actual insight itself are two fundamentally different things. So having similar experiences yourself does not at all mean that you are having an insight or that you will have an insight. When the time is ripe, when you are ready, you will have your distinct experiences and your own distinct insights. Then you will understand the vast difference between whatever you have read or heard about insight and the actual insight. You can express the effect an insight has on you or the experiences 'around' it but not the depth of understanding you gain through the insight.

Such a direct experience of reality will have a profound impact on your practice, on the way you perceive the world and on the way you lead your life. In other words, the wisdom you acquire in this way will immediately alter the way you see things. However, an 'insight-mind' is not permanent; it only lasts for a moment. What perpetuates, what remains 'alive' is its quality, its potential. Unless we keep nurturing this quality it can fade away. Only continued practice will keep it alive, will make sure that the wisdom you have acquired keeps doing its job and that you keep growing in wisdom. Continued practice does not mean you have to spend a certain number of hours per day or per week sitting in meditation, even though it certainly helps. Continued practice means being mindful in whatever you do, to the best of your abilities.

At this stage of the practice, wisdom is moving into the limelight. Awareness remains as always at its side but now wisdom is running the show. This kind of wisdom will help us make significant progress in our practice.

Sutamayā, cintāmayā, and bhāvanāmayā paññā also work hand in hand. The wisdom you gain by thinking will increase your faith in the Dhamma and therefore further stimulate your interest in the practice. Increased interest in the practice will result in more learning and thinking. You will stop being afraid of making mistakes and will start exploring new ways of dealing with difficulties. You will see the benefits of the practice more clearly and understand what you have learned at deeper levels. All this will further increase your faith. Once you start having insights your faith in the Dhamma will get a tremendous boost. This will yet again strengthen your determination to practise wholeheartedly. The practice of mindfulness will become the mainstay of your life and your world will never be the same again.

No matter how experienced you are, no matter how much more knowledge you have than everyone else, never be satisfied with the wisdom you have acquired or with the depths of insight you have had. Do not limit yourself; always leave the door wide open for new and deeper understandings.

Food for Thought

The following points were brought up during many Dhamma discussions with dozens of yogis. Some of them were beginners, others were already very experienced practitioners. Depending on your personal level of meditation experience, you may or may not understand some of these points. Don't worry about those you don't understand yet. Just allow them to sink in. Over time, as your practice unfolds, their meanings will become apparent and you will understand them at deeper and deeper levels. As your meditation progresses, you will eventually understand them all. These points are not arranged in any particular order, so just read a few at a time whenever you feel a need for some input or for some inspiration.

1. Meditation is not just about sitting on a cushion. No matter what posture you are in, if your mind is aware with understanding, you are meditating.

2. If you can't observe, don't force yourself to do it. Learn how to relax, how to be comfortable first.

3. Try lying down meditation every now and then. Learn to develop awareness in whatever posture you are in. Always remain aware of your experience and notice the difference in mental effort needed to maintain awareness in different postures.

4. Right effort means perseverance. It does not mean focusing hard, controlling, forcing or restricting yourself. Focusing hard arises from greed, aversion, or ignorance of the practice.

5. You can be aware of bodily sensations, mental feelings, and mental activities. But do not think of them as 'mine'; they are just what they are: sensations are sensations, feelings are feelings, mental activities are mental activities – that is their fundamental nature. Always try to observe them with this view in mind; if you don't, i.e. if

you experience them as 'mine', attachment or aversion will inevitably arise.

6. Learning to observe, investigate and understand the nature of an object is more important than just wanting to see it disappear or trying to make it disappear. Wanting the object to disappear is wrong attitude.

7. When there are no defilements in the watching mind, you have right mindfulness.

8. The knowing mind (*viññāṇa*) is the mind that cognizes whatever comes to the sense doors. It is always present but it can neither recognize nor interpret; it has no wisdom, no understanding of what is going on. The knowing mind simply senses objects.

9. The observing or watching mind observes whatever you experience. When you are aware that you are observing, you are aware of the observing mind.

10. You can only become aware of the mind through the presence of its activities and feelings. Whenever you are aware of thinking or that there is anger, disappointment, desire etc., you are

aware of the mind. You need to recognize that it is the mind which is doing or feeling all this.

11. When you interfere with the watching mind, insight cannot arise. Learn to watch objectively, with bare attention.

12. When you observe your mind, you will be surprised, amazed and possibly even shocked to discover fixed ideas, wants, fears, hopes, and expectations which you have not been aware of.

13. All worldly activities (e.g. reading, listening to music, playing sports) involve thinking and conceptualizing. Without it, external stimuli (objects) become meaningless. But if conceptual thinking comes up during meditation, you should simply be aware that 'the mind is thinking'.

14. When you can easily stay with an object it is either because of the gross nature of the object, or because your mindfulness is strong. Don't be content with observing gross objects only. Your mindfulness will become stronger as you learn to observe subtle objects.

15. The moment you start disliking someone, an imprint or data is created within your mind. The

imprint then causes you to see that person in a fixed way and prevents you from seeing how he or she really is. This is delusion at work.

16. When the mind is ready for insight, it will arise naturally, spontaneously. Don't look or hope for insight to arise. Looking for it will lead to false creations of the mind.

17. Always keep an open mind about whatever you experience. Try not to jump to conclusions. Simply keep observing and investigating your experience thoroughly and continuously. Jumping to conclusions will prevent your understanding from deepening.

18. If you keep avoiding difficult situations, you cannot learn and grow. This is especially true for dealing with the defilements. Learning to face the defilements allows you to investigate and understand their nature, and this will help you to transcend them.

19. Learn to be interested in difficult situations. By being present with them in a gentle manner, you may suddenly understand what caused them.

20. Feelings need not be identified or categorized as pleasant, unpleasant, or neutral. Remind yourself

that a feeling is just a feeling. Accept it just as it is.

21. When watching a movie, all members of the audience will perceive it in their own way, from their personal perspective. Those with a relatively immature mind may view the movie as pure entertainment. Those with a more mature mind will also try to understand the message in it. In meditation too, you should always try to understand what is happening.

22. The more you concentrate or focus on an object, the more energy you use. This makes the practice difficult and tiring. Your mindfulness may actually slacken. When you then become aware of this, you will probably try hard to build up the level of mindfulness again. Which, of course, means using even more energy, and this snowball effect burns you out during a long retreat.

23. When you put in too much effort to be mindful, you will spend your energy too quickly and therefore you will not be able to maintain mindfulness throughout the day. If you practise in a relaxed way, you will conserve energy and be able to practise for long periods of time. If you

are a long term meditator you cannot afford to waste your energy. Meditation is a life long undertaking; it is a marathon, not a 100 metre dash.

24. See each and every moment as a valuable opportunity for the development of awareness but do not take the practice too seriously. If you are too serious about it, you become tense and are no longer natural.

25. Once you know how to relax, you become sensitive to your own needs. You will then know when you are using energy unnecessarily, and also learn to conserve your energy.

26. After you have heard or read about other people's meditation experiences, you might, consciously or unconsciously, be on the lookout for them. Then if you experience something similar, you might jump to the conclusion that it is an insight. But you have only had a similar experience. An insight is true understanding of reality.

27. The wandering mind is a natural mental activity. If we keep pushing it away we are not accepting what's natural. Once we accept this, i.e. have the right attitude, watching the wandering mind becomes easier. In the beginning you may often

lose yourself in thought, but that is okay. Over time and with practice, you will start observing the wandering mind as 'just thoughts' and get lost in it less and less often.

28. Don't resist, don't expect – accept things as they are.

29. The wandering mind is not the problem; your attitude that it should not be wandering is the problem. The object is not really important; how you observe or view it is important.

30. What you are observing or where you are observing it is not important; your awareness of it is important.

31. Every moment is the right moment for meditation.

32. The purpose of samatha is to attain certain mental states, whereas vipassanā is a journey of learning and understanding.

33. Mindfulness meditation can be compared to watching a movie. You just sit back, relax and watch. The storyline of what you are watching will naturally unfold – and how much you learn from what you watch depends on your level of understanding.

34. If you don't have the right attitude, then one way or another, your mind is defiled.

35. Insight per se is not so important; what is really important is whether or not the insight leads to a transformation in your mind which will enable you, in future, to handle similar situations without defilements.

36. When there are defilements in your mind, you have to recognize and acknowledge their presence. But it is also important that you are aware of the absence of defilements!

37. Understanding is not linear. You can understand things in different ways, on different levels and from different angles.

38. Wisdom inclines towards the good, but is not attached to it. It shies away from what is not good, but has no aversion to it. Wisdom recognizes the difference between skilful and unskilful, and it clearly sees the undesirability of the unskilful.

39. Delusion can cause you to see things upside down; it makes you see what is wrong as right, and what is right as wrong.

40. Avoiding difficult situations or running away from them does not usually take much skill or effort. But doing so prevents you from testing your own limits and from growing. The ability to face difficulties can be crucial for your growth. However, if you are faced with a situation in which the difficulties are simply overwhelming, you should step back for the time being and wait until you have built up enough strength to deal with it skilfully.

41. The purpose of practising is to grow in wisdom. Growth in wisdom can only happen once we are able to recognize, understand, and transcend the defilements. In order to test your limits and to grow, you have to give yourself the opportunity to face the defilements. Without facing life's challenges, your mind will remain forever weak.

42. Developing awareness is a life long journey. There is no need to hurry or worry. It is important to practise in the right way, so that whatever you learn will be useful in daily life, not just in the meditation centre.

43. The more you try to see something, the less clearly you can see it. Only when you are relaxed

can you see things as they are. Those who don't try to look for anything, see more.

44. Strong mindfulness is not some kind of power. Mindfulness is strong when the defilements are not present, when you have the right attitude.

45. Know what attitude you are observing with. Observing alone is not enough.

46. If the pain you suffer from is caused by a physical injury or disorder – be careful not to aggravate it.

47. Sometimes, when things become difficult, the mind is reluctant to observe or practise. Depending on your ability and state of mind either continue to be aware or just stop and rest mindfully.

48. In life you should learn not to expect anything in return for whatever you do for others. With the work of awareness too, you should learn not to expect any results or good experiences.

49. It is of utmost importance to recognize pride in order to weaken it and prevent it from growing stronger. Wisdom can only arise when pride is put aside.

50. Holding on to a preconceived idea or view of what insight should be like is dangerous, as it leads to pride when you have an experience that seems to fit such an idea. The nature of reality is beyond ideas and views. Ideas and views are merely the work of delusion.

51. Don't confine the practice to the retreat centre; apply it in daily life. When you leave the retreat, take the practice with you.

52. When the mind is strong and comes into contact with an object, it does not judge; it understands the object just as it is.

53. Try to observe how the mind deals with a difficult situation as often as you can, from as many different angles as possible. Once you have developed an understanding of how the mind works in this situation, wisdom will naturally begin to do its work. Next time you are faced with a similar difficult situation, wisdom will prevent you from reacting in an unskilful way. Wisdom knows what to do.

54. When you start to watch thinking, you cannot recognize it as the mind. You are only aware of thinking and the contents of thinking. Through

practice, through repeated looking at thinking you will get to understand that it is the mind that is thinking. This is not easy to describe in words. But once you are able to do this, you can observe the mind objectively. You just recognize it as thoughts that appear in the mind. Learn to acknowledge thoughts whenever they arise. Don't try to avoid doing this by keeping your awareness on the body only; you may miss the nature of how the mind works.

55. When your mindfulness is strong and continuous, you will naturally start watching subtle objects. Being able to stay with subtle objects causes the strength of mindfulness to increase further, thus enabling you to watch even more subtle objects. The ability to watch subtle objects develops gradually; you will not achieve it by forcing yourself to be mindful or by trying hard to watch them. (Note: Strong mindfulness is used to describe a state of mind in which the Five Spiritual Faculties of faith, effort, mindfulness, concentration, and wisdom are in balance – a state of mind that has been developed through the momentum of persistent practice.)

56. It is not difficult to be aware or mindful. It is difficult to maintain it continuously. For this you need right effort, which is simply perseverance.

57. To be relaxed and in the right frame of mind is of prime importance. Everything else comes later. To recognize whether or not you are in the right frame of mind is more important than experiencing peaceful states or having a 'good sit'.

58. If you are sleepy every time you sit, you have developed a bad habit. So when sleepiness begins, open your eyes. If it persists, get up and walk. It does not matter whether you sit or walk; it is important that the mind is awake.

59. Right effort is reminding yourself to be aware. Right effort is not about using energy to focus on an object.

60. If tiredness sets in towards the evening, you possibly used excessive energy during the day. Your practice should gain momentum; you should not suffer from exhaustion. So don't use excessive energy trying to be more mindful; simply keep reminding yourself to be mindful.

61. When you close your eyes to meditate, you may get the impression that there is suddenly a lot of

thinking. But the mind is actually thinking all the time. You just do not notice it because when your eyes are open you are paying more attention to external objects than to thoughts.

62. To be able to maintain any skills you have acquired, you need to continue practising them. So keep up your meditation practice. Try to practise wherever you are, as much as you can. Keep persevering and don't let what you have learned go to waste.

63. If you are aware, just be glad that you are aware. That is the right attitude. So when you are confronted by a defilement and are aware of it, be glad that you are aware of this defilement, even if it does not seem to dissolve. As long as you are aware of the defilement, you are doing well.

64. Defilements are part of the Dhamma. Do not reject them. A yogi got disappointed when the defilements quickly disappeared. Not that she wanted the defilements but she was very keen to learn from them, to understand them. This should be your attitude when you are faced with defilements.

65. Try to recognize that defilements are simply defilements; that they are not 'your' defilements. Every time you identify yourself with them or reject them, you are only increasing the strength of the defilements.

66. Always remember that it is not you who removes defilements – wisdom does the job. When you are continuously aware, wisdom unfolds naturally.

67. After someone has stolen something from you, don't try to tell yourself that you don't really mind and that it was a form of giving. That is a trick of the mind. Recognize and accept your annoyance! Only if you can watch your annoyance directly and understand it, will you be able to totally let go of it.

68. The experience of calmness is not so important. It is more important to know and understand why calmness does or does not arise.

69. To know reality you have to be courageous. If you wish to arrive at the truth you have to start meditating, to be aware of yourself. The first thing you need to acknowledge is that there are defilements in your mind. This is basic. We all

want to be good and we therefore tend to see and show only our positive sides. If we do not face the defilements we end up 'lying' to ourselves and others. If you want to change for the better you must know your negative sides. When you start seeing yourself in a realistic way and acknowledge both your good and bad qualities, you are doing well.

70. The Buddha did not say that we should not think, talk or act; what he said was that, instead of being driven by the defilements, we should apply wisdom when thinking, talking, and acting.

71. When you are in conversation you have the habit of putting your attention outside, of getting involved with the topic of conversation and the people you are talking to. Most of the time you are too concerned with other people's emotions. Train yourself to continuously look inwards; you will naturally become more and more skilful at it. Also train yourself to remain aware of your attitude. Only to the extent that you are no longer emotionally involved in the conversation will understanding arise. You will begin to recognize your limits, know when it is time to stop talking,

know what you should or should not talk about, and know how to communicate without getting involved emotionally.

72. When you are watching an object, you should check the awareness again and again. Doing so allows you to become aware of the awareness of the object – learn to observe the watching mind.

73. Once you become more experienced in meditation, you will start thinking that you understand what it is about. But jumping to such a conclusion will prevent you from deepening your understanding.

74. When your experience in meditation widens and deepens, you will tend to make conclusions about the nature of your experience. You may even assume that you have understood a fundamental truth, such as impermanence. This kind of assumption will prevent you from looking deeper and will hinder further progress.

75. If you are able to notice subtle impulses in the mind you will also see their subtle motivations and realize that most of these motivations are defilements.

76. Do not decide how long you are going to sit; that will create time stress. Do not take the schedule at the retreat centre too seriously. Simply remind yourself to maintain awareness in all postures as continuously as possible.

77. When you are eager to make progress you will not be fully aware of the present. That is why it is so important to keep checking your attitude. A yogi once said he had realized that his eagerness to apply right attitude continuously was a wrong attitude!

78. Every intention comes with a motivation. Most motivations are defilements. Only if you fully recognize and understand defilements, wisdom will arise. Now wisdom will motivate your intentions.

79. Intentions do not only occur at the beginning of every movement or action. There are intentions throughout each movement or action. Even every moment you are sitting has intentions. It is important to remember this.

80. Once you see the danger of the defilements you will always want to keep the mind in the most positive state possible.

81.   It is the nature of the mind to be constantly in contact with objects, so you do not have to make a special effort to see an object. Just become aware of what is there and do not try to see what you think is the right object. There is no need to control or to manipulate your experience.

82.   When people start meditating, they tend to have fixed ideas of how the practice should develop. But you do not need to do or create anything. You just need to develop continuous awareness, to watch and observe. That's all. You cannot make things happen, but when you develop awareness correctly, things will happen. The same is true for the arising of understanding, be it simple or deep, even enlightenment!

83.   You can only work on the causes, not on the results. You cannot achieve what you want by just aiming for it. For example, it is not possible to develop concentration by just trying to concentrate. You need to know how concentration is developed. When mindfulness is continuously applied with the right attitude, concentration develops. You can actually only remind yourself to be mindful and check whether you are doing

it with the right attitude. In other words, if you have right effort and right mindfulness, right concentration will come naturally. If you understand cause-effect relationships you will know how to deal with any situation. Always ask yourself if you know the causes and conditions that are necessary to achieve the result you want. Then work on fulfilling those causes and conditions. You need to have this right view.

84. Right mindfulness is not forgetting to be aware of the right object; right effort is to persevere; right concentration is stillness or stability of mind. The right object is your experience, for example the emotion of anger – NOT the person you are angry with.

85. Do not practise too seriously, but peacefully and respectfully.

86. If you think that you are watching the same thing over and over again you will become bored. However, if you take a closer look at your experience you will understand that no two moments feel exactly the same. What makes you feel bored is thinking that you are watching the same thing. In fact, nothing is ever the same,

every moment is always new. Once you can really see this, your mind will always be interested in whatever it observes. No moment will ever be boring because your experience will clearly show that 'things' are forever changing.

87. Thoughts influence the way you feel. How you view what you are doing is very important.

88. Someone who has understood the benefits of the practice will never stop practising. Those who stop have simply not understood the practice fully.

89. Whenever you get this feeling of not knowing what to do, just wait. Don't do anything.

90. Mindfulness is when the mind is full of awareness!

91. Awareness needs time to develop. In the beginning you have to keep reminding yourself to be aware, but when the momentum picks up you will remain aware naturally. You cannot force the awareness to become strong. Only by being aware continuously, momentum will be gained.

92. When the mind is pure, peaceful and equanimous, you will immediately notice any bodily

tension caused by the arising of even very subtle defilements.

93. In order to understand defilements, you have to watch them again and again. What can you gain from just having or expecting good experiences? If you understand the nature of the defilements, they will dissolve. Once you are able to handle defilements, good experiences will naturally follow. Most yogis make the mistake of expecting good experiences instead of trying to work with the defilements.

94. Sometimes you may feel that being aware of certain objects is a waste of time. This idea is totally wrong. The key to the practice is the awareness itself, not the object. As long as you have awareness you are on the right track.

95. Learn to watch defilements as defilements and not as 'I am defiled'.

96. The quality of awareness should be accepted as it is. Problems arise when you have a preconceived idea of what awareness should be. If you do not accept the quality of your awareness, you have a wrong attitude and are most probably trying to have an imagined experience.

97. If you want to find the right balance you have to experience and understand the extremes.

98. You do not need strong effort to be mindful. When we are present, we become aware of what is happening. Simply reminding yourself to be in the present moment is all the effort you need to be mindful.

99. Once awareness gains momentum, being aware of the awareness will sustain the momentum.

100. When the mind is calm and peaceful and there is no obvious object to observe, take the opportunity to recognize the quality and strength of awareness of that moment.

101. If you become mature in your practice, you will be able to handle difficult situations simply because you understand the conditions behind them. Understanding the conditions enables you to work on the cause. Why not take difficult situations as learning opportunities?

102. It is important to notice assumptions. Assumptions are based on wrong views, and they will prevent you from seeing the true nature of things.

103. Vipassanā always steps back to see things more clearly, whereas samatha dives in and gets absorbed in the object. Stepping back and watching allows understanding to arise.

104. In the beginning you start off by just being mindful. Once you become skilled in consistently bringing the mind to the present moment, you can start to observe or investigate what you are aware of.

105. Thinking is within the mind. Peace too is within the mind. Understanding this allows you to watch them as mind objects rather than as something personal, as 'mine'. If you do not see peace as simply a state of mind, you will be drawn into it.

106. Checking your attitude is also awareness.

107. If you lose the desire to meditate or feel you do not know how to meditate, do not panic, do not try to make yourself meditate. Just remind yourself to relax. The desire to meditate will naturally come back after a while. Trying hard will just make things worse.

108. When a sense of resistance arises in the mind, learn to feel it directly.

109. Many people are reluctant to work with the bad experiences they have in their meditation. You can usually learn more from bad experiences than from good ones; in fact, very deep understanding can arise from working with bad experiences! Learn to accept both good and bad experiences.

110. It is important to have some theoretical knowledge, but you should hold it lightly. Beware of jumping to conclusions when you have an experience that seems to match the theory. Once you truly understand something experientially, you will see the vast difference between your initial interpretation of the theory and actual understanding.

111. You can only observe what you are experiencing in the present moment. You can neither observe what has not yet happened nor what has already passed.

112. Do not participate in what is happening. Learn to just be aware of it.

113. If you are aware of your awareness, you are meditating.

114. Let the mind naturally choose its object. You just need to be aware of the quality of your awareness.

115. If you are experienced in watching your awareness, you will be sure of its presence and, whenever you lose it for awhile, become aware of its absence.

116. Though it may be difficult for you to practise awareness in daily life you should still persevere. Sooner or later, even a small effort in mindfulness will make a noticeable difference in your life.

117. Looking for something which we think we are supposed to see is not mindfulness meditation. Mindfulness meditation is just being aware of whatever comes your way.

118. When you observe something, don't identify with it; don't think of it as 'I' or 'mine'. Accept it simply as something to know, to observe, and to understand.

119. The work of awareness is just to know. The work of wisdom is to differentiate between what is skilful and unskilful.

120. Real acceptance and detachment are born of wisdom.

121. Whenever you have wisdom you are aware; but just because you are aware does not necessarily mean you have wisdom.

122. Always make it a point to check your attitude before you do sitting meditation. Be simple. Just sit and watch what is happening. Is it difficult to know what you are doing right now?

123. In the beginning wisdom comes a little later than awareness. However, over time, through practice, when you have developed wisdom, it arises simultaneously with awareness.

124. When things are good, learn how to detach from them. When things are not good, learn how to accept them.

125. In the beginning of the practice you may feel that there are too many things you need to watch, but when there is momentum everything seems to slow down and you will have enough time to watch it all, to see more details. It is like watching a moving train. If you stand close to a railway line watching a train move past you at high speed,

you will mainly see movement and hardly any details of the train. But if you are on a moving train yourself and another train travels at a similar speed parallel to the one you are in, you will not see the train in its entirety but you will have enough time to see details.

126. If you are aware of your facial sensations during your sitting you will be able to know whether you are relaxed or not. When you are focusing too much it will show on your face. When a person is really relaxed, the face is very clear, soft and calm.

127. One thing you need to remember and understand is that you cannot leave the mind alone. It needs to be watched consistently. If you do not look after your garden it will overgrow with weeds. If you do not watch your mind, defilements will grow and multiply. The mind does not belong to you but you are responsible for it.

128. Excitement weakens mindfulness.

129. Lobha is an unwholesome volition, a defilement. Chanda is a wholesome volition, an expression of wisdom.

130. Be aware of peacefulness. Be aware of the aware-ness of peacefulness. Doing so allows you to check whether or not you are indulging in it, getting attached to it, or still aware.

131. When expectations arise in the mind, learn to see their nature. Every time you are upset or dis-appointed with someone, whenever you feel any resistance to the way things are, you can be sure that you have expectations.

132. Do not be led by greed. Take time to learn a little about greed. Pay attention to its characteristics. If you keep falling for greed, you will never understand its nature.

133. Many people believe that strong mindfulness is a kind of power. Actually, strong mindfulness is simply an awareness that is free from anxiety, expectations, or wants – a mind that is free from concerns, that is simple and content. When you have these qualities, you can actually feel an increase of mindfulness. Strong awareness does not come about by trying very hard or trying to focus intently.

134. When you try to get rid of thoughts you are actu-ally trying to control them rather than learning to understand them.

135. When your understanding of the true nature of things grows, your values in life will change. When your values change, your priorities change as well. Through such understanding you will naturally practise more, and this will help you to do well in life.

136. When you learn to talk with awareness in a relaxed manner, mindful of your intentions, your way of talking will become less emotional.

137. Only when you are ready and able to watch difficult emotions are you able to learn from them.

138. A wise and skilful person can turn poison into medicine. A skilled meditator can transform hindrances into understanding.

139. Throughout our life we habitually seek and grasp. To sit back and just watch this happening is difficult. However this sitting back and just watching is essential to become able to see and understand these habits.

140. When there is attachment or aversion in the mind, always make that your primary object of observation.

141. Only if the mind recognizes a wrong attitude can it switch to the right attitude.

142. When you are in a positive frame of mind, it is important to recognize it. Recognition tends to strengthen this wholesome state of mind.

143. Check your attitude before you attempt to watch sleepiness. If you resist it, meditation becomes a struggle. If you accept it, you will find it easier to make an effort to be aware.

144. To be able to observe things as they are without labeling is more real and effective.

145. If you are continuously aware of your state of relaxation you will become even more relaxed.

146. If you feel happy and at peace with yourself when you are on your own, make sure to check your attitude. If you become attached to solitude without being aware of it you will easily become agitated when your solitude is threatened.

147. If you target an object you complicate your practice. Targeting a particular object means that you have the fixed idea that this is the right object to observe for a set period of time. If your mind then turns to other objects, i.e. does what is natural instead of obeying your fixed idea, you will become agitated and disillusioned.

148. You should not be concerned whether you have good or bad experiences. You should only be concerned about your attitude towards these experiences.

149. When you start practising you have to keep reminding yourself that thoughts are just thoughts, feelings just feelings. As you become more experienced you will gradually understand the truth of this. But as long as you keep identifying with your thoughts and feelings, i.e. if you keep clinging to the view 'I am thinking' or 'I am feeling', you will not become able to see things as they are. You cannot see reality if you have a wrong view, if you see things through a veil of ignorance.

150. If you are aware of whatever you are doing, the mind will know its own limits.

151. When we think, speak or act with defilements, we will find ourselves again and again in saṁsāra. In the same way, when we think, speak or act with wisdom we will find our way out of saṁsāra.

152. If you are dissatisfied with your practice or if you are practising too seriously, you will not experience joy and calm.

153. If the mind is dissatisfied with the practice it is likely that you want something. You might then try to force the practice. This is not helpful.

154. If you do not understand the practice you will not be happy to practise.

155. Right practice brings joy and interest. Right practice brings benefits and the potential for living a meaningful life.

156. If you understand the practice and its benefits you will never have a boring moment.

157. It is perfectly natural to become sleepy. If you feel bad about sleepiness it means you have an aversion towards it and you will try to resist it. This is a wrong attitude. Simply recognize and accept sleepiness. As long as you observe sleepiness with the right attitude, you are meditating.

158. If you have no money you cannot become a businessman. You have to work hard if you want to make a living and save up some money. If you then invest this money wisely you will make more money. Similarly, when you are new to mindfulness meditation, you will often find it hard to practice continuously and to acquire

some wisdom. If you know how to apply the wisdom you have, you will develop more wisdom.

159. In vipassanā the object serves as a means to help us develop right awareness, concentration and wisdom. If the mind reacts with any kind of defilement (*lobha*, *dosa*, or *moha*) you have wrong awareness and so concentration and wisdom cannot arise.

160. Do not try to avoid objects or experiences, try to avoid getting entangled in defilements.

161. You need to understand that everything that happens is just a natural manifestation of cause and effect. First try to accept things the way they are and try to see that 'this is not me', that this is just 'nature' at work. You need to acquire this kind of wisdom first. It is this wisdom that can eradicate the defilements.

162. Samādhi is not about being focused. Experiencing samādhi means the mind is still, stable, and calm.

163. The samatha yogi deliberately chooses an object. The vipassanā yogi observes what is happening and is therefore aware of many different objects.

The samatha yogi gets attached to the object. The vipassanā yogi does not get attached to any object. Wisdom can only arise when there is non-attachment.

Keep Practising

The Satipaṭṭhāna practice can be applied in daily life. It is not difficult at all. People find it difficult only because they lack sufficient practice. It is important that you make a sincere effort in your practice. Through experience you will see for yourself that it is really simple. If we had the same attitude of perseverance and untiring effort towards the practice as we have towards our careers or business matters, this would come easier.

Unfortunately, most people believe that they do not have enough time to nurture and value the Dhamma; they are ever so busy making a livelihood. But you should not worry about making time to practise; simply remind yourself to be aware while you are going about your daily activities. Be patient in acquiring the right views, the right understanding, as well as the necessary skills. If you practise wholeheartedly and persistently you will sooner or later experience benefits.

Once you truly understand the benefits of the practice you will never stop practising; you will always keep it going wherever you are. When you are really able to apply the Dhamma in your life and start seeing the difference it makes, then the qualities of the Dhamma will become obvious. The qualities of the Dhamma will come alive for you, they will become really meaningful to you.

A meditation centre is just a place for learning, a kind of training camp or mindfulness workshop. Keep practising in daily life. Do not think it is difficult. Just try again and again. Developing awareness is a life long journey; there is no need to hurry or worry. It is important to learn how to practise correctly so that you can effectively apply whatever you have learned in everyday life. When you are able to apply what you have learned in any life situation, your awareness is superior to the kind of awareness you develop by just walking up and down the meditation hall.

You will be happier and get on more harmoniously with other people if you are clearly aware of whatever you do, wherever you are. This only comes easily when there is sustained momentum in the practice; it only becomes possible when there is natural awareness, when awareness becomes second nature.

When you have a new experience in the course of your practice, do not try to interpret it in the light of what you have heard or read. If the understanding you have gained through the experience is real, insight or wisdom will bring about a real change in your views, habits, ideas, even your behaviour. What is the value of insight if it does not help you change for the better?

What is the Right Attitude for Meditation?

1. Meditating is acknowledging and observing whatever happens – whether pleasant or unpleasant – in a relaxed way.

2. Meditating is watching and waiting patiently with awareness and understanding. Meditation is NOT trying to experience something you have read or heard about.

3. Just pay attention to the present moment.
    Don't get lost in thoughts about the past.
    Don't get carried away by thoughts about the future.

4. When meditating, both the mind and the body should be comfortable.

5. If the mind and the body are getting tired, something is wrong with the way you are practising, and it is time to check the way you are meditating.

6. Why do you focus so hard when you meditate?

Do you want something?
Do you want something to happen?
Do you want something to stop happening?
Check to see if one of these attitudes is present.

7. The meditating mind should be relaxed and at peace.
   You cannot practise when the mind is tense.

8. Don't focus too hard, don't control. Neither force nor restrict yourself.

9. Don't try to create anything, and don't reject what is happening.
   Just be aware.

10. Trying to create something is greed.
    Rejecting what is happening is aversion.
    Not knowing if something is happening or has stopped happening is delusion.

11. Only to the extent that the observing mind has no greed, aversion or anxiety are you truly meditating.

12. Don't have any expectations,
    don't want anything,
    don't be anxious,
    because if these attitudes are in your mind, it becomes difficult to meditate.

13. You are not trying to make things turn out the way you want them to happen. You are trying to know what is happening as it is.

14. What is the mind doing?
Thinking? Being aware?

15. Where is the mind's attention now?
Inside? Outside?

16. Is the watching or observing mind properly aware or only superficially aware?

17. Don't practise with a mind that wants something or wants something to happen. The result will only be that you tire yourself out.

18. You have to accept and watch both good and bad experiences.
You want only good experiences?
You don't want even the tiniest unpleasant experience?
Is this reasonable?
Is this the way of the Dhamma?

19. You have to double check to see what attitude you are meditating with. A light and free mind enables you to meditate well.
Do you have the right attitude?

20. Don't feel disturbed by the thinking mind. You are not practising to prevent thinking, but rather to recognize and acknowledge thinking whenever it arises.

21. Don't reject any object that comes to your attention. Get to know the defilements that arise in relation to the object and keep examining the defilements.

22. The object of attention is not really important, the observing mind that is working in the background to be aware is of real importance.

    If the observing is done with the right attitude, any object is the right object.

23. Only when there is faith or confidence (*saddhā*), effort will arise.
    Only when there is effort (*viriya*), mindfulness will become continuous.
    Only when mindfulness (*sati*) is continuous, stability of mind will become established.
    Only when stability of mind (*samādhi*) is established, you will start understanding things as they are.
    When you start understanding things as they are (*paññā*), faith will grow stronger.

Glossary of Pāli Terms

During Dhamma discussions you will hear both the teacher and the interpreter use certain key Pāli terms. They are usually left untranslated because translations can only approximately describe their meanings and can sometimes even be misleading. The explanations given should be sufficient for our purposes but they are not comprehensive. For more complete definitions please consult Buddhist dictionaries and textbooks. Also try to get a 'feel' for these terms when you hear them used, try to understand them in context.

abhidhamma	Buddhist canonical description of the processes and characteristics of the mind
akusala (also see *kusala)*	kammically unwholesome, unskilful, unprofitable
anatta (also see *atta)*	a) not-self, non-ego, impersonality, there is no abiding substance (or an ego, a self, or a soul), there is no self-existing entity
	b) nothing can arise on its own or from a single cause, and nothing can exist or move on its own
	c) one of the three universal characteristics of existence (see *dukkha* and *anicca*), understanding anattā is a liberating insight (*paññā*)

anicca	a) impermanence, all conditioned phenomena are impermanent, everything that comes into existence changes and passes away
	b) one of the three universal characteristics of existence (see *dukkha* and *anatta*), understanding anicca is a liberating insight (*paññā*)
atta	self, ego, personality
avijjā	synonym for *moha*
bhāvanā	mental development, meditation
bhāvanāmayā paññā	wisdom or knowledge acquired through direct experience, through mental development
bhikkhu	fully ordained monk, member of the Saṅgha
cetasika	mental factor (This refers to the 52 mental factors listed in the abhidhamma. Some are kammically neutral, some kammically wholesome, some kammically unwholesome.)
chanda	wholesome intention, aspiration, zeal
cintāmayā paññā	wisdom or knowledge acquired by thinking and reasoning, by intellectual analysis

citta	mind
dāna	giving, offering, generosity
dhamma	object, thing, phenomena
Dhamma	a) 'natural law', 'nature' b) Buddhist doctrine
diṭṭhi	view, belief, speculative opinion *micchā diṭṭhi* (wrong view) / *sammā diṭṭhi* (right view)
domanassa	any kind of unpleasant mental feeling, mentally painful feeling
dosa	hatred, anger, any kind of aversion or disliking (including sadness, fear, resistance, etc.)
dukkha	a) unsatisfactoriness, pain, suffering b) the suffering in change c) the unsatisfactory nature of all existence, of all conditioned phenomena d) one of the three universal characteristics of existence (see *anicca* and *anatta*), understanding dukkha is a liberating insight (*paññā*)
indriya	the 5 spiritual faculties: *saddhā, viriya, sati, samādhi,* and *paññā*
jhāna	meditative absorption

kamma	volitional action (of body, speech, mind)
khandha	5 aggregates or categories: *rūpa, vedanā, saññā, saṅkhāra, viññāṇa*
kilesa	defilements, unwholesome qualities of the mind, any manifestation of greed, anger, and delusion (see *lobha, dosa,* and *moha*)
kusala (also see *akusala*)	kammically wholesome, skilful, profitable
lobha	greed, any kind of craving or liking (synonym for *taṇhā*)
mettā	loving-kindness, selfless love, unconditional love
micchā diṭṭhi	wrong view
moha	delusion, ignorance, not understanding, not seeing reality (synonym for *avijjā*)
nāma	mental processes, mind (collective term for *vedanā, saññā, saṅkhāra,* and *viññāṇa*)
nāma-rūpa	mental and physical processes
ñāṇa	synonym for *paññā*
Pāli	name of the language in which the Buddhist scriptures (Pāli Canon) were first recorded

paññā	wisdom, understanding, knowledge, insight (synonym for *ñāṇa*)
paññatti	relative (conceptual) reality, concepts
paramattha	ultimate reality
pāramī	perfections
paṭicca-samuppāda	dependent origination, conditioned co-production, conditionality
pīti	joyful interest, enthusiasm, rapture
rūpa	physical processes, corporeality
saddhā	faith, confidence, trust
samādhi	calmness, stillness or stability of mind
samatha	tranquility meditation, concentration meditations
saṁsāra	cycle of suffering
saṅkhāra	mental formations
saññā	recognition, memory, perception
sati	mindfulness, awareness
sīla	morality, ethical conduct, virtue
somanassa	any kind of pleasant mental feeling, mentally pleasurable feeling
sukha	happiness

sutamayā paññā	wisdom or knowledge acquired through reading or hearing
sutta	discourse of the Buddha
taṇhā	synonym for *lobha*
upekkhā	a) neutral feelings and sensations (*vedanā*) b) equanimity, a wholesome mental state (*saṅkhāra, cetasika*)
vedanā	pleasant, unpleasant, or neutral feelings or sensations (see *somanassa, domanassa,* and *upekkhā*)
vinaya	rules of conduct and discipline for monks (*bhikkhus*)
viññāṇa	consciousness, cognition, knowing mind
vipassanā	insight, insight meditation
viriya	energy, 'wisdom' energy, 'remindfulness'
yoniso manasikāra	a) right attitude, right frame of mind, right attention b) wise consideration